Love Kept Hope Alive

Love Kept Hope Alive

Freda Harrison

ARPress
ILLUMINATING IDEAS.
EMPOWERING VOICES

ARPress
45 Dan Road Suite 15
Canton MA 02021
  Hotline: 1(888) 821-0229
  Fax: 1(508) 545-7580

Ordering Information:
Quantity sales. Special discounts are available on quantity purchases by corporations, associations, and others. For details, contact the publisher at the address above.

Printed in the United States of America.

ISBN-13:   Softcover   979-8-89676-457-1
                 eBook   979-8-89676-458-8

Library of Congress Control Number: 2025919520

Contents

ROSE
LOVE

AND NOW ABIDETH FAITH, HOPE, AND LOVE THESE THREE. BUT THE GREATEST OF THESE IS LOVE (1ST CORINTHIANS 13:13)

THE ROSE CONTINALLY BREATHES THE MARVELOUS GRACE OF GOD.

It is with a heart of gratitude that I dedicate
this book to my mother, Chola Enda Keith,
and to all caregivers of Alzheimer's patients.

Freda Harrison

Introduction

A DAUGHTER/NURSE STRUGGLES FOR the care of her mother with Alzheimer's. I have heard many times from preachers to teachers, there are two ways to walk in life: wisely or unwisely. My mother would always say, if you're going to do something, do it right the first time and you won't have to redo it.

When caring for a human life, you really need to make wise decisions and let the doctor in on all that's going on with that person, because if the doctor doesn't know, he or she won't be able to help. The following story is my family struggle with Mom's Alzheimer's. As you read this book, I pray for joy, peace, and blessings to all, because there is a higher power.

This is a picture of an American Flag, that
we saw flying for the 4th of July to honor America
May God Bless America and all that the flag stands for.

For God was pleased to have all his fullness
Dwell in him making peace through his blood
Shed on the cross.

Colossians 1:19-20

1.

I WAS RAISED IN a small laid-back little town called Pine Hollow, Blue Ridge. I was the oldest of seven children; four girls and three boys. I became interested in healthcare at a very young age. My father came back from the war (World War II), all messed up, body and mind. I can remember, my father getting big bags of medicine from the Liberty Veterans Medical Center. Sometimes this medicine had an awful effect on him. He wasn't himself when he took these meds.

I can still remember the nightmares that my father would have at night about his buddies, getting blown to pieces and his cry out to God. I have some very good memories of my dad. He really did believe in God and I have heard him pray and ask God for something and it would be given to him. Most of my father's kin were Seventh Day Adventists. When Dad took us to church, he chose Baptist and the Church of God.

In December of 1965, I had a sister, named Briarwood, she was so beautiful, fair skin, yellow-blonde hair. She looked like an angel. She died from a tragic fire accident. My dad prayed and cried to God if he would send him another baby girl like Roselyn, that he would always serve him. For the next year, Dad and Mom took us to church, most of time it was a Church of God. Almost one year after my sister's death, God gave my dad what he asked for. I was young, but I knew then that the person upstairs was real. My dad was so very happy and his faith very strong. I remember him taking Bible lessons from Walter Dean Calloway and was so proud of this. But as my father's health declined, the hospital visits became more often and the medicine more.

Dad was in the Veterans Administrations Hospital in Ashford, Blue Ridge. He had run away and they sent the police to get him. In Whitely City, this police officer had been in office a long time, and everyone loved him. His daughter was the schoolteacher. She happened to be my schoolteacher that year. When I came home from school, my mom was at work. She had taken a job taking caring for this friend of ours who needed help and didn't have anyone to help her. I saw this police car in front of the house. My dad was at the front door, with a gun aimed at the police.

I threw my books down and started crying and went over and stood in front of the police and started saying "No Daddy, please don't!" It was by the grace of God that he put the gun down and told the police how sorry he was, that he didn't want to go back to the veteran's hospital. The police told him that he had to go back.

Sometime after, he had gotten out and lost his mind, and beat my mom and tried to kill all us kids, but by the grace of God, we all lived, but things didn't get better for my father. He had run away again from the Liberty Veterans Medical Center. He came to Northshore, where my mom and my siblings were with me. The police got him and put him in the state hospital there. And he found a way to hang himself. In a way, my mom, and all of us kids were at peace and he would never hurt anyone again and at last my father was really at peace. The picture below is me and my sister Roselyn, taken before her death.

Freda and her sister Roselyn, taken in 1963.

2.

Picking Up the Pieces

MOM AND MY siblings stayed in Northshore for six months then wanted to return back to Pine Hollow, Blue Ridge. It was the spring of 1971. I remember, when we got home, that this was the first time we had been there since Dad's passing. Our house had been broken into and almost everything that was worth anything was gone. I can remember my mom breaking down and crying. We all did, but crying did make us feel better; but we knew that we must pick up the pieces and go on. In cleaning up, we found some traps that my father had sat to kill us, like shotgun shells turned upside down in an innerspring mattress, and a large ashtray with a broken, sharp edge. It was then that I knew that my dad was really a very sick man, and that it was by the grace of God, putting his angels around us, that was keeping us from harm.

Mom did very well. She got a job at the Cumberland Falls Restaurant as a cook, and worked very hard to make ends meet and fix what was left of our home. She cleaned houses for the elderly, and took them to doctor appointments. She started a game room called Pine Hollow Game Room. She also had a snack bar in it. I went to visit Mom a lot there. I noticed that she was doing a great service. There she gave teenagers moral support if they were going through a rough time. Some of these young people would tell me how wonderful my mom was, and how she had helped them.

I was there one evening and this girl was crying and I overheard her say to my mom that no one cared about her, and my mom, told her, "I do. I love you, and God loves you." I thought what a great service my mom was doing. Mom really did enjoy helping people, young or old.

3.

Freda and her mother on her wedding day

A MEMBER OF OUR church at Parkers Lake Chapel got sick with cancer, and my mother took a job taking care for her during the day, while her husband ran a gas station. She got very close to her and when she passed away, my mom took it very hard. She had taken care of her for almost one year.

Anytime anyone in our family got sick, they would always call on my mom, because they knew she was very good at taking care of the sick. She was a very good nurse without a license. I remember from early childhood, when we all would have the flu, Mom would call Dr. Halvorsen, and he would bring us antibiotics and Coke. Mom, with her eighth grade education, knew how to follow directions on what the doctor said. I still remember my mom fixing catnip tea. She would go to the woods to get this and boil it and if we were sick to our stomach, it would help.

I remember one weekend, one of my sister's husbands was in the army and coming home on leave. All of us went to meet him at the East Valley Regional Airport. My sister's mother-in-law had gone with us. We were sitting in the coffee shop of the airport. We were sitting in a booth; I was on the end. We had all ordered coffee. When the waitress brought it, she poured all the coffee out on me. Mom got so mad she told that waitress that she ought to know better. She made me go to the bathroom to see how badly I was burned. Thank God that back then the coffee wasn't as hot as it is today. It hurt and I was very red, but not blistered.

I can remember Mom coming to Northshore when I was very sick with gallstones and taking care of me. She also took care of an aunt, who had a stroke, for almost six months. My mom's oldest sister had a heart attack and she stayed with her for almost one year. Before my aunt passed away, she redid her will and left my mom with life insurance and her savings account and her house and all the belongings. Mom did not want to stay in Northshore so she chose to sell everything at auction and return to Pine Hollow, Blue Ridge.

4.

Slipping Away

IN THE EARLY eighties, I went home to visit Mom. We stayed up late talking, but after we had gone to bed, I got up and noticed that Mom's light was on. I went in to see what she was doing and she was sitting in the middle of her bed with a box of letters. She said, "I really should throw these away." It was letters from my dad; some had been written when he was in the veterans' hospital and some were from when he was in the war. We sat and talked for a while. I knew that night that she really love my dad. She wondered why he did all the bad things he did. All I could really say was that only God knew for sure.

It was shortly after this, I saw things going on with Mom. Whenever we would go for walks or shopping, she would get out of breath. The doctor told her that sixty-five percent of her breathing had gone from her lungs. He ordered her oxygen by nasal canula at two liters as needed. She took this really well. That year, I remember buying her a dress with daisies on it because she had grown the most beautiful patch of daisies that I had ever seen.

I noticed that her medicine wasn't being taken right. She had stopped cooking and cleaning. She was having hypertension problems. I noticed that she was buying things from the store, such as fat burner pills, and all kinds of sinus medicine. Primatine pills and the inhaler. She told me she was taking a blood pressure pill with a water pill in it, for a sleeping pill.

My baby sister had to call the drug store to see if I was telling the truth. Then they took her to the doctor to get her medicines straightened out.

Two years later, I noticed that Mom stopped grooming herself. I went home one weekend and found her very dirty and smelling badly. I asked if any of my sisters had been there. My brother, who never married or left home, and stays with Mom, told me that none of them had been there. I bathed her and then called my sisters and asked if we could all work together to help Mom. I explained the condition I found Mom in. She took good care of us; we need to take good care of her.

I asked to put a volunteer book there and told them if they would see about her through the week, that I would do the weekends since I live out of state.

They did not want to do this and it had really made them mad that I had asked such a question. Their reply to this was, "Mom doesn't want anyone to do anything for her. She says she is just fine."

But before I came back home, they all were letting me know that I was not Mom's nurse.

I stayed away for two months, figured I had caused enough trouble. My brother, who lives with Mom, called and told me that when I cross state lines to please leave the nurse behind. Because the nurse was not welcome.

I came back home praying and asking God, "You chose for me to be a nurse and I could have chosen any field of nursing but my love was for the elderly." One of my favorite childhood memories was when my father's family would have get-togethers at Daniel Price, my great-grandpa's house.

While the other children were out playing, I was sitting quietly on a footstool by Great-grandpa. This gave me so much joy. My father's aunt Cole was a surgery nurse in Clearwater, North Carolina. I can remember back not paying any attention to what the grownups were saying, but really enjoying my time with Great-grandpa. Then I started asking myself, is the love of my job and the love from helping others going overboard? I feel I am really lucky to work at one the nicest healthcare facilities in Magnolia. It's a team effort, from everyone, from doctors, management, families, nurses, can's When I see how well our Alzheimer's patients are managed, with the proper treatment, it makes me so sad that a lady who gave so much of herself is getting very little or no proper medical care for her condition. It's sad and such a shame. This is my mom, who took wonderful care of me. I don't think I am wrong to want good care for her. If my siblings could show me a paper that Mom had signed, saying, "I don't want proper healthcare if something happens or to not bathe me if I get unable to bathe myself. Let me rot and stink," but I know there is no such paper. My mother always took pride in how she looked.

I went back two months later to give Mom a perm and do her nails for her birthday. I stopped at place called Papa's Pizza and got a pizza so we would not have to cook. My brother met me at the door and told me I would have to bathe her before we ate. I told him no problem. She smelled so bad. She had not had a bath in two months, since the time I had been gone. Mom had three pairs of pants on. I had to count to ten. I told my brother if I ever caught her like this again, I would bring her back to Magnolia with me. I was also mad at him. How could he have the nerve to stay there, day in and day out, knowing she needed help? He is getting the house. What makes him think it's not his job to keep her clean?

Before I left, I called my sisters to see if we could get home health to come and help her. Then, they all got mad at me for asking such a question. My brother let me know that no one strange was going to come in the house, but, the last remark was, "Freda, if you pay for this, bring it on. We don't want Mom's money spent on her care."

I came back to Magnolia, trying to figure out why my family didn't want my mom to be taken care of. I was so broken-hearted, I had to look to God for peace.

The next thing I noticed was that her memory was getting worse. She was seeing and hearing things that weren't there. I asked my sister if they had told the doctor, and she told me that she was trying to look into what was wrong with Mom, and I should take one day at a time. I am sorry, but I could not make any sense of this. She also explained that Mom's memory problem had to do with her not wearing her oxygen. I went home to see Mom one Friday afternoon.

My sister had just come back from the doctor with her. She said that the doctor was taking her off her inhalers because she was abusing them. He said it was worse for her to have them and abuse them than not to have them at all. Of course, my family did not agree with this. This also explains the hearing and seeing things that weren't there.

This was the fall of the year. I hoped that my sister, who took Mom to the doctor, would do some research on this, since she worked at the health department. I did not say much more. But I prayed to God to please take care of my mom, because as a nurse, I know how hard it is to come off a drug that has been abused. And Mom was getting to the point it was hard for her to express what was wrong with her or how she really felt. I asked everyone I knew to help me pray for her.

The next time I went home was Christmas. We were at a dinner and gift exchange. When I went in, Mom was sitting at the dining room table. She was holding her head. I said to Mom, "You look awful." She stated that she felt awful too. My brother told me that she had been to the emergency room the night before for high blood pressure. I didn't say anything, because I had prayed all the way there for God to help me from not letting the nurse in me come out. I wanted so bad to have a nice time with my mom.

I walked into the living room to put gifts under the tree, and what I saw next made the nurse in me come out. I saw four or five Primatine mist inhalers, and Primatine pills, plus some sinus medicine. I called my sister, who took Mom to the doctor. I told her all this over-the-counter medicine was as bad (or worse) than what the doctor would give. Her reply to me was,

"This opens up her lungs so she can breathe." I told her that this will kill her. She told me that they would be over in a few minutes. I took Mom's blood pressure; it was 190/100. Two of my sisters came in at the same time. I told them what her blood pressure was. One of my sisters stated that the blood pressure was much better than the night before.

They all started yelling and telling me again that I was not Mom's nurse. I tried to get them to have a family meeting, away from Mom. They would not agree. I told them that it was shameful they weren't getting her treatment for Alzheimer's so this could be managed.

Then, they all took their turn at me, even my sister's daughter. "Freda, you are looking for a miracle and there's no miracle." Then I heard, "Mom is going to die. Let her die in peace." Mom started to cry. Then my sister's daughter looked at me and said, "Now, look what you have done." I was in shock. I could not believe that this was my family. My sister, who is a schoolteacher and the wife of a Baptist preacher, put her hands on her hips and she said to me, "Freda, if you want to quit your job and come and take care of Mom, come on, but I don't think that's what Mom wants."

I reminded them that I loved my mom and I wanted to have her as long as God would let us have her, and that God is the giver and taker of life. I went into the living room and grabbed up all the inhalers and sinus medicine and headed back to Magnolia. I cried and prayed all the way back home. This time, I really knew that my poor mother was really in need of a miracle, so I started praying, asking everyone I knew to help me for her.

When I got back home, I contacted social services in that area. They went out and did some education with my brother. I sent the inhalers to her doctor along with the sinus medicine. I was hoping that he would do some more education with my sister when she took her back, but, he told my sister that to find her another doctor, that he wasn't going to doctor her anymore. I really felt bad about this. My sister told me how ashamed they all were with me. She told me to find Mom a doctor and start taking her. I agreed to do this. I went down to only working Monday thru Thursday so I would have Fridays free to take Mom to the doctor. I found a doctor for Mom and made her this appointment. I took a few days off from work. By this time, she really needed to go to the doctor because was having chest pain.

I got there on Thursday and her doctor's appointment was Friday morning at 9 A.M. When I got there, my brother told me that he was not going to give my mom any medicine from this doctor. And of course, my mother heard what my brother said, and she said, "I am not going to see no doctor." I could not believe this. Here is a brother who lives with Mom, who doesn't think it's his place to make sure that Mom is clean, not wanting me (who is a nurse) to not take my mother to the doctor. Things just didn't make sense then. But now, I believe that he thought I would leave Thursday after he told me he wasn't going to help me take her to the doctor, or give her medicine. But I had taken days off from work and wanted to spend time with my mom. Several times during the night, he reminded me I wasn't Mom's nurse.

When we got up Friday morning, at 8:30 A.M., Mom got up and was having chest pains. My brother gave her a breathing treatment with her nebulizer. Then one hour later, mom came through the hallway. She held her chest and begin to yell, "Oh! Oh!" My brother ran for the breathing machine. I saw how wild she looked in her eyes, sucking real hard on the mouthpiece. I didn't say a word. I ran outside on the porch, crying. My brother followed me out there. I looked him in the eyes, and said, "My God, Mark, do you know what you are doing? You are killing her. You are causing her chest pain. This is an overdose and abuse effect." I told him I was going to leave and that I would be calling social services again. I let him know that I did not like what he was doing to my mom. I didn't try to call my sisters to talk about this. The greatest one I got to talk to is God. Social services weren't too friendly with me. I think they went out with a nurse, and did some education with my brother. This seemed to help. Her chest pain stopped, she was seeing things less often, she was even breathing better.

5.

Don't Know What to Do

I PRAYED EACH AND every day that God would put his
angels around my mother and keep her from harm. At this point, I
knew the dangers around her, and knew that God was the only answer.
The burden I was carrying was so big and heavy, and at work, I would
see families working together for their parent's care.

I would say to myself, "I wish my family could come together and
all of us be involved and wanting the best care for Mom."

Mom seemed to be getting better, since the abuse of the breathing
treatments stopped. I give thanks to God.

Mom when she visited dad's grave in Northshore

Freda her mom and son Evan taken at Lake Erie in Port Clinton,
Northshore

6.

Over the Next Hill

I WAS SO HAPPY. Mom had been getting along well, able to walk without chest pain. It was now November. I was planning on going up and doing Mom's hair and giving her a perm. I was talking to my sister-in-law and she told not to plan on it because one of my sisters had Mom's hair cut off real short, like a man's. This didn't make any sense to me, because they all know that I do Mom's hair. I went up to see Mom, but I didn't get a perm to put in it. Her hair was very short. I made the comment that me and Mom should do this to who did it to her. She laughed and said, "Yes, we should." I took supper in that night and I hadn't been there long when I found out why my sister got Mom's hair cut off. Mom went to the bathroom and came out with a wet towel and wet washcloth. She had the towel around her neck and the washcloth she was rubbing her face with it. My brother said that she had been doing this for three weeks. I asked him if he had told the doctor and he said that he had spoken with someone one the internet on Pal Talk, and that this was normal part of the Alzheimer's. I explained to him that the doctor needed to know. I also was telling him some things that he could do to keep her from doing this and I told him that she was going to get really sick if he didn't keep her from doing this. He was very quick to tell me he wasn't going to do any of these things. Because he would have to go out of his way to do them and Mom also had a bump on her head, blue in color. I asked how she got that, and he said that she tried to get in the car and bumped her head. I also told him he needed to go to Lowes and get some door alarms, for her safety. He told me that he heard her every time she moved, and that he wasn't going to do that either.

I didn't go back for a while, but I called often. My brother would always say she was fine. I called on February 14th at 8:30 A.M. my brother said Mom was running a fever and he thought she had pneumonia from going outside with the wet towels and washcloths. They admitted her and kept her for two days, then sent her home with some medicine. The next weekend, I had made some things for my sister's craft store and took them up. I had a sore throat and had not planned on going near Mom, because if I had strep, she didn't need it on top of pneumonia. My sister said that they had to stay around the clock with her because she was unable to walk. I told her that I would stay that night with her. When I got there, she was asleep. She woke up an hour after I got there. She walked into the living room where I was. She was walking just fine and sat down beside me and was talking fine. My brother told me that it was time for her medicine and I told him that I wanted to get her to eat something first. I fixed her some scrambled eggs after asking her what she wanted and she was unable to tell me. She ate well. Then I gave her the meds my brother handed me to give her. It was about one half hour later, that she was unable to talk to me and she could not walk. I told my brother that this was not right. I called the hospital emergency room and they ask why someone hadn't noticed this sooner instead of giving this all week. I explained to her that I was from out of town and I didn't know the reason they hadn't noticed this. She said stop giving it and see our family doctor on Monday.

I stayed all night that night. By morning, Mom was moaning, in a fetal position, and running a 102 fever. I woke my brother and told him that Mom needed to go to the hospital. He called my baby sister, and she came over and called the ambulance. They found out that she had low potassium and bronchitis. They gave her IVs and sent her home with some medicine.

I had to go back to Magnolia, but I called often. It was going to be Mom's birthday soon and her hair had grown, so I took a perm and had her birthday party and dinner. When I got there, she was sitting at the dining room table with a wet towel around her neck and a washcloth, rubbing her face. I took her to the bathroom and fixed her hair before the birthday party and dinner. We had a very good time. But before my sisters left, I asked if we could talk about how we could keep Mom from the wet soaking towels. They really didn't want to talk to me about this. We were going to move the towels and my brother got mad about this. Then my baby sister told me not to contact social services again, and my brother told me that they asked him the last time they were out if he wanted to get a restraining order to keep me away. My baby sister said, "Freda, do you think Mom would like to live like this?" What planet are these people on? Mom is very much alive, and that's not for them to choose. I am sure none of us would want to live like that, but does that mean we should not have proper healthcare, or even comfort care? The sister who said this to me was the one who when she was born, my friends would come home with me to see her, and Mom would only show her from inside the screen door. Why do none of my siblings seem concerned about Mom? They should not be talking about her dying in front of her.

None of us is promised tomorrow. Each day is a gift from God. I pray for God to send a miracle of love to my family. Because when you love someone, you really care for them, and want the best for them. God touched me that night, and I knew I must lay this all down at the feet of Jesus, even though the human part of me didn't want to, because I love her so much. There was some peace and I knew God and his grace would help me get through this, but I felt as if I had just walked away from a gravesite. Still, with a great deal of sadness, but also with the calm assurance that my mom would be okay, at last, that there wasn't anything else I could do but lay this all down at Jesus' feet.

Freda and mom on her 74th Birthday

Mom's 74th birthday cake.

Z.

The Awakening

WHEN I GOT back home, I went to visit the Alzheimer's Association and they gave the phone number of the Blue Ridge Association, who gave me a phone number for the Blue Ridge Legal Aid for the Elderly. He gave me the following information:

1. He stated that there is no law to make my siblings be wiser and take better care of Mom.
2. My family does not have to take better care of Mom.
3. He stated that with social services being against me, if they wanted to, they could get a restrainingorder to keep me away.
4. With HIPPA laws, they don't have to tell me anything about my mom.
5. He also said that my sister, who has control of Mom's money, doesn't have to spend it on her, andif she lived to the point of a nursing home, the money will be all gone. In most cases, this was how it was.

8.

A Daughter/Nurse View

GOD HAS TO really help me each and every day with being a nurse and not being able to help your own mother, and not understanding why they don't want me to help with her, and why they don't want to do better by her is not clear to me. There is so much help out there for her and for them, but they have to want it. I feel that by them not getting her proper treatment they are cheating her (and all our family) of some time with her.

I will always look up to God, and he will give me comfort and peace. For he is bigger than any problem that we may have.

The Hawthorne sing, "God on the mountain is still God in the valley, God of the day is still God in the night." I think of how wonderful God is and the blessings he gives each day. Then I hear a small still voice saying. "Look upward." I am, God. "I will take care of your mother."

2.

Best Mom

DEAR GOD, THANK you for giving to me the most wonderful mother that anyone could have. I will always remember the good times, and also the bad times, because they made us stronger.

1. I am so grateful that I got my love for doing and helping people from you, for there is no greaterjoy and blessing than from helping others.
2. Mom, you always said it is better to give than to receive. Thank you for teaching me that.
3. I am so grateful I got my love of flowers from you. How can anyone see and smell beautifulflowers and not think of Jesus?
4. Mom, most of all thank you for just being you.

Freda and mom at Morehead Lighthouse
in Morehead, Northshore on Lake Erie

10.

One Oct. day (Oct. 2005)

I WAS WORKING ONE evening and a coworker brought some pictures that she and her Husband had taken of their family. I told her that I would love to have some pictures Taken of me and my mother and she said "Go ahead and do it." I thought it over and called mom Ask her if she would come to Ga. with me if I would take the rest of my vacation days? Of course talking to mom, was by then off the wall, but I talked to my brother who lived with my mom and explained what I was wanting, to do. He stated that this would work out great because they needed to get some work done on the roof of the house, and that She would not understand the noise. I called the photo shop in our area mall and they were taken fall and Christmas pictures the booking was almost, no openings but there One 30 min. Opening available. I took it because I really wanted these pictures. I explained about my mother having Alzheimer's she also told me those 30 minutes was not Long that we might not get many pictures but I still wanted to try.

I had spoken, to my brother couple weeks before this because my mom had been sick was running a temp and I told him to take her to the doctor, and I called back ever night for a week or more worried about my mom. He had a reason ever day why he didn't take her. (1) Couldn't get her to go. (2) I didn't have time. (3) I will take her tomorrow. I explained that it could be dangerous if infection got into bloodstream this could kill her. I ask why my sisters 3 of them that lived close by wasn't helping with her he stated that, "they were all busy, I will take her tomorrow". I called him the very next night to see if he took her. He told. Me that he took her to the emergency room and couldn't get her out of the car. The emergency room staff had to help get her out it took them over an hour he said. They ran Test and she had a bladder infection it was really bad. The doctor explained, to him the importance of getting her to the doctor before it gets this bad and that this could lead to death. I explained the importance of taking the medication just as the doctor told him.

Mom had already taken all of the antibiotics by the time I wanted to go get her for a few days and take our pictures. Dear God. What is wrong with these people I am a nurse, Taking care of the elderly is all I have ever done it's been my life. I am a very caring nurse and my years of nursing gave me lots of knowledge but I can't even help my own mother.

I took my vacation days and went to Blue Ridge, to get my mom, for our pictures and to spend a few days together. When I arrived it was 1pm on Wednesday afternoon Mom was sating on the porch looking for me. She was so glad to see me. I was glad to see her to. My brother told me that she had taken all of her medication and he didn't send any with her. We got back to Magnolia at 6pm we talked the whole time back most of it off the wall but so what this is my mom, and such a joy she was.

I noticed that mom had lots of anxiety and I also noticed that she was having trouble When she would lie down I had to put lots of pillows to prop her up so she could rest. The next morning at 10am we had an appointment for our pictures. I got her ready but me was worried because she seems to be having more anxiety than before. I really wanted these pictures and I prayed to God, to please help me out here with my mom. Then we headed to the mall. When we got there the photographer saw how much anxiety my mom had and explained that her next person came in we would have to stop. I told her that I understood and it would be fine 1 or 2 pictures will be ok better than nothing. The photographer was taking pictures left and right. The next person didn't show up and she took some good shots. The pictures were nice. I thanked God for answering my prayer. I told my mother, mom. You have just give a daughter the most precious gift that you could ever give a daughter, she said what I gave you I said these pictures.

Mom got worse with anxiety and I had nothing to give her. I called my brother and Told me that he gives her bendy. I explained to him in the elderly that it can cause more anxiety. I gave her 25 mg bendy this did not help like I told him it cause more anxiety. She was up all night. I took her back home the next morning because I knew she needed Medication I didn't have and needed to be seen by her doctor.

When we arrived to Blue Ridge, with her one of my sisters who works at the health dept. Was there very upset that I had brought her back acting as if she really cared I will take her to the doctor and see if what you gave her was really a bendy. If she cared where was she at a few weeks ago at this point I don't think mom, is nowhere well something is wrong. I was nice to my sister, I told her I love my mom and yes, bendryl was all I gave her.

11.

I got to find a way to help mom

As I MADE my way back to Magnolia, I kept thinking, dear God, there's got to be a way for me to help my mother. We had never had a family meeting on taking care of mom. I had called my sister who is a school teacher and a wife of a baptist preacher and her thing was mom, didn't want us to do anything for her. I told her if they would take care of her during the week I would do the weekends but they wanted the nurse to but out and stay out.

The nurse in me knew that something was bad wrong with my mom. And if I was going to do something I better do it now, and not be playing. So I planned to take some time off work to go get her if she would come to Magnolia. I called and found this Doctor who would admit to nursing home near my house so I could be close by. To my knowledge no one in my family has power of attortany over her. Years ago my sister who works at the health dept. told mom, that if she got sick and needed someone that she would quit Work and take care of her that's how she got our old homeplace she never kept her word. This was my plan if I could pull it off. I would call all of my family when I had gotten emergency power of attorney.

I called my brother and talked to mom, and ask her if she would stay a week or so with me and she told me that she would. I went the next morning and got her. When I Arrived there she was sating looking out the window for me with tears in her eyes and I asked what was wrong and she replied, 'I told Mark, that it was a shame as sick, as I am And it was just me and him,' I gave her a big hug and kiss and told I was here things Was going to be alright. I ask my brother for her insurance cards since she was going a week or so. I ask for her small oxygen tanks. The only meds he sent was a low dose ativan. I had an appointment 10am the next morning with the doctor. She didn't rest good so I gave her ativan that he had given me. It didn't help. When I got her to the doctor's office I couldn't get her out of the car. Office staff had to help it wasn't an easy task but they finally did it. When the doctor Came into the room she said that mom, would need to be in the hosp. that she had a bad case of congested heart failure. She called an ambulance and took her. They put a foley cath in and got 2,000cc of fluid. I was so thankful that I went and got my mom, because she would have been dead in a few days. She also still had a kidney infection. I was going to call my siblings and tell about mom, but I wanted to wait till I had emergency power of attorney but someone Called thinking they was doing a great thing and by the next evening they were calling me not wanting to know how mom was but bottom line they had hold of what they Wanted was mom's money. I went and got papers from court so I could get her treatment. I told the doctor that after she got on her feet I was taking back to Blue Ridge When mom, was released from hosp. She was put in a nursing Home near my house I was there ever day to help with her, mom, was doing real good eating getting therapy Taking medication that she needed. I was so pleased.... .

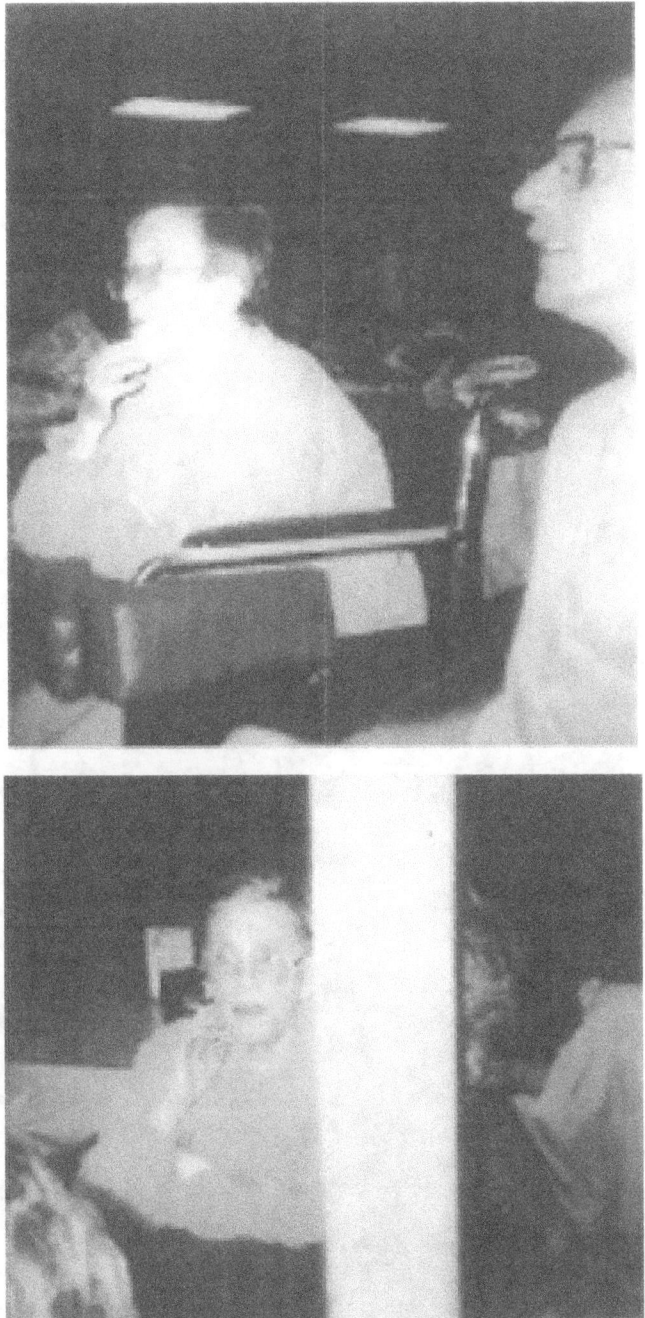

This was me and my mom, taken before my siblings took her to Blue Ridge. She was never able to talk or walk again we had a great time that night.

12.

It will all come out in the wash.

My mom used to say when she couldn't figure things out that it will all come out in the wash. She taught us as children to not hide or try to cover up something with a lie because it would always caught up with you and you will have egg on your face. Being Honest is always the best because you can't hide it from God and after while there is a Pay day ahead.

After a few days in the nursing home my mother was doing fine. Walking with help. Talking, eating with help and taking her medication for me I was the only one to get her to take her medication mom, was even singing amazing grace with me I was so happy such a good outcome.

After a few days my attorney called and said that 'my sisters had hired an attorney and that they had faxed them {from all three sister's power of attorney.} He said we would have to go to court so it was arranged the following Wednesday.

The night before court the following day all of my brothers and sisters except the one Who had lived with mom, they came to the nursing home where mom, and I were and Not wanting to see how she was but to tell her that tomorrow she would be out and they Would take her home to, Blue Ridge. They even brought my x husband of 20 years. I could not believe this. Mom and my x husband who never got along. All looking like they could kill me.

I ran out side and sat on a bench out front and was crying so hard with pressure on my chest. I could not believe this, then my brother, from Brookhaven, Blue Ridge came to tell that I wasn't his sister any more and that why didn't I call him and I tried to explain but he didn't want to hear it. He looked at me and told me that I needed help and he hoped I got it. I told him that God was on my side and that I knew that all of them would be together but that God would be with me. This is a brother who has so much education but no common sense. They all left after making their show and we all met in the court room the next morning.

My sister who is a school teacher told the judge that she had taken good care of our Mother, had a bunch of papers in her hand that she had gotten from past doctor visits. And that she was a school teacher and a wife of a Baptist preacher and a good citizen of my community. My sister who works at the health dept. told the judge, that my mom never liked me and that she didn't want me to have any kind of saying about her health care. The judge, ask her if she had something in writing to that effect. She told him no. Then she ask, him if she could get an order to keep me away from my mom? He said NO.

He told them that since all three of them had power of attorney, that they could take her back to Blue Ridge, but that she would have to go right into a nursing home. My sister who is the school teacher, told him that she had a promise of one in one month. The judge said no that it would have to be tomorrow. You never saw fingers pushing numbers on a cell phone so fast in less than a few minutes. She had placement in Sunrise Manor, the same one I was going to put her in when she had gotten on her feet. The Judge talked to nursing home to confirm placement then he talked to my family and told them that she was to go, home with my sister Clara, who worked at the health dept. and, the next morning to be taken to Sunrise Manor, in Riverton, Blue Ridge. The judge also said that he was going to have the doctor who was taking care of mom, talked to them about her care and medication she was on and why.

The doctor, came in never missed anything, she covered how sick my mother was when she started taking care of her. How important oxygen was at this point, and that She was on 2 liters all the time. And how important all the medications were that she was also explained that some of them could not be stopped cold turkey, and needed tapered off. After the doctor talked to them then the judge said that we could be dismissed and that could go get my mom, and transport her to Blue Ridge.

13.

Saying Good bye to mom

Iᴛ WAS NOON, when we all left the courtroom, them to get mom, and me to say goodbye. I had mom's small oxygen tanks in my car and I told my sister who is teacher and wife of a preacher and such a good citizen of where she lived. She had small oxygen tanks that they might need them, she said, 'No, thanks all I want is mom, you keep them.' I thought they may have some more in their car. I all so offered to help get mom's belongings But she said, that she didn't want them

My brother from Brookhaven, Blue Ridge, was in the dinning room with my mom, along with my brother in law, who works at the welfare office with no social work skills. They informed me that they were taking mom with them after she finished eating. I ask where my sister who, was so caring before the judge and he said that she was at the hosp. to get her records of what had been done to her.

It was noon and by leaving at this time they would hit rush hour in East Valley, Tenn. It was a five hour drive. I gave mom, a kiss and hug and told her I loved her. The nurse came over and told my brother that the wheelchair she was sitting in, and the oxygen Tank she was using belong to the nursing home and would need to be brought back in.

Below is how my mom, looked when they left with her. She was talking even singing Amazing grace, walking with help, eating with assistance. I went and got mom's things Out of her room then I went back home.

14.

Visit at Sunrise Manor in Riverton, Blue Ridge with mom.

Mom, LEFT MAGNOLIA with my brother for Blue Ridge and this was the following Saturday I decided, to go see her and take her things that I had thinking of The oxygen tanks that might be needed as I got there My brother, who lived with my mother was standing out side smoking. I told him I had mom's belongings and he said that mom, was not the same person and I wanted to know why and he stated, "my, sister who took mom, home to her house didn't come get her oxygen tanks and she had stroked out on the living room floor and an ambulance had to be called." I could not believe this, after the doctor talked to them on how important all of this was to mom's well being. What planet did they come from?

Where my sister lives it's a 45 min drive for emergency personal to get to you. AS bad this was I knew I could not say anything after all she was now in a place she should be and I had to go on.

My brother was right she wasn't the same person that left Magnolia. Mom, was unable to talk. Unable to hold her head up right. Unable to sing unable to look around and notice things. Thank you God, that I don't have that memory of my mother stroking out because I wouldn't give her the care she needed when I was told in a court of law. How important it was. I knew that Mom, was God's child and all these people will pay for this.

I made my visit short and gave her a hug and kiss and came back to Magnolia. Hating the Condition, I found mom and the reason why but my faith in God gave me comfort and Peace knowing all I could do was pray and let handle it.

15.

Oh, no where is mom

AFTER ABOUT A week I thought I would call the nursing home where mom was at and see how she was doing. When I called they told me that she wasn't there. I asked where she was and they stated that they couldn't tell me they told me to call my family. I didn't know what was going on or where she was.

I called my brother in East Valley, Tenn. and they had put her in Cumberland County Medical Services. I was ok with this because I had worked there at one time and it is a good nursing Home. I still didn't pick, up on anything going on and no one said anything so I figured that I would go up the next couple of weeks to see mom.

By this time it was the second week of November soon going to be Thanksgiving, I had took a few days off from work and went and got a small Christmas tree and thought that just maybe this would brighten mom up.

One of my friends told me to not go by myself that she would go with me. So we took off the next morning to see my mom. When we got there I went and ask where mom's room was having my things I had gotten for mom. When I walked in her room there was an empty bed. Then in walked a nurse and told me that mom, was in the hosp. in Hillsboro, Tenn. Then there walked in the administer of the home he had a paper in his hand and told me that he hated to be the one to tell me but there was a court order and I couldn't see my mom. I ask him to let me see the order he said "he couldn't but I could go to the court house and get a copy. "so that was what I did. I still could not believe this my baby sister Rebecca Lawson, had gotten it stated that she believed that I was a threat to my mother.

I cried with the order in my hand all the way back to Magnolia, I know my friend with me was afraid for both of us she prayed for Jesus, to help us he did he took the wheel and got us back home safe because I was in no condition to drive I was in a daze.

When I got back I called all of them Rebecca, wouldn't even talk to me and the others talked to me so mean my sister who is married to the preacher hung up on me each time I called.

I tried real hard to put this in the hands of the Lord. My doctor sent me to the hosp. Because the chest pain was so bad I couldn't stand it I was having trouble breathing I Failed the stress test given by the, doctor. Everything about my heart was ok, so he referred me who treated for anxiety I was under her care for a long time.

I was getting better still wanting to see my mom, but I prayed to God, that he would give her hugs and kisses for me. My brother in East Valley told me that she had gotten Out of the hosp. and was back at the nursing home.

16.

Hospital visit in Hillsboro, Tenn.

MY BROTHER WHO lives in East Valley, Tenn. and told me that mom had been taken back to hosp with kidney failure and that they didn't give her much hope. I ask if I could see her. He said, "I don't think that they will be anything said about it. He gave me her room number. I took another day off from work and went up to see her.

When I got there it was around 1pm. My Sister, the school teacher was sitting on the Lounge chair, watching TV and playing with her beautiful hair. My mom was in a fetal Position, with hands folded up to her neck with a painful grip. Moaning going from one Side of the bed, to another. I felt of her as the nurse and the daughter would do. She was very hot not warm but hot. I ask my sister, "When is the last time mom, had something for pain or fever?" She didn't know so I went out to nurses' station and ask if mom could have something for pain and fever? The nurse told me that she would see. When I got back in the room my sister had gotten up from her lounge chair and got over in the only chair that was by mom, it was plain to see she didn't want me to get near mom. She said to me. "Freda, I have about had it with you. I have power over mom's care and I don't want you to say anything. Is that clear? All that I could say, was you should have been a nurse not a school teacher I knew that I must be going because I felt like moping the floor with my sisters pretty hair. I all so knew that this was what she wanted me to do. Because they would love for me to lose my nursing license and this would be one way to do it. I prayed with mom, and told her that if I never seen her again I would meet her in heaven and I left crying and praying again to God. I saw my brother who had lived, with mom out in the parking lot. He never said one word to me, I was unable to Speak. I got in the car and headed back to Magnolia. Crying and praying to God, to please protect my mother from her children.

17.

Court again

WHEN I ASK God, to protect my mom, he truly did and I thanked him so much she was now back at the nursing home. My brother in East Valley, Tenn. Called and told me. I was still missing her so bad it was the 1st week of Dec. I had already bought her Christmas presents and wanted so bad to give them to her but couldn't.

Around the second week of December. There came a letter from my sister, Clara who worked at the health dept. Telling me that she loved me and that families should love Each other unconditionally and that they were going to have a Christmas party at the nursing home where mom, was at. And that they wanted to invite me to join in on the Joy of the holiday season. I was so happy I thought this is a prayer answered. I called my friend and read her the letter she said "Freda, I don't want you, hurt any more than you are, why don't you call the administer of the nursing home and ask him/" I took her advice and called, it's a good thing I did because, here is what he told me. He said that got a new order and the new order reads, that I may come and see mom, but I would have to stay 1500 feet away from her He, said that he was sorry but that was what the new order read.

I called my sister Clara Mae Collins, and ask her why she had done this to me? Are you trying to kill me? She could give me no reason why but she did this tried to say that the State welfare I called around and ever one said that it wasn't them.

I decided to get me an attorney to see if I could get to see my mom. We sold a boat so I could get the money. It didn't do any good bottom line, and I knew it they all three had power of attorney and if they didn't want me to see my mom, I couldn't see her. But I had to try. Because I love my mom so much and I know that she would try for me.

In the End I know that God, will be the final judge. He will take care of all these Cural and evil people it will come back home to them.

18.

Slipping in to see mom.

AFTER GOING TO court and trying to get to see my mother failed. I knew that I must Do what I got to do I knew that I loved her and a team of wild horses couldn't keep me away. I had to do the only thing left to do. I had to slip in ever chance I could and offer to help with her care. I took a camera with me and snapped pictures and sometimes I would get told to leave then I would leave but I would already have gave her a kiss or Done her nails and took plenty of pictures. The times I got told to leave my heart was broken but I understood. Each time I slipped in I had pictures that I took. Sometimes if a certain nurse was there she would stay close by and let me give her a bath and change her Sheets. What a joy to this for my mom. I prayed that God, truly bless that nurse. She was truly a good nurse.

This was how my visits with my mom, was sometimes good if I didn't get ran out. I was there one Sunday, and my baby sister the one who got the court order that I was a danger to my mom, Rebecca Lawson. She and her wonderful husband walked in and I Was doing mom's nails they didn't say a word. They stood at the foot of her bed for almost 15 minutes or 20 minutes. Neither one of them said a word. Then all of a sudden they walked away. Then about 10 minutes, the nurse came in and told me that I had to leave I know on her way out she called and got me threw out. I was thankful for my time with my mom.

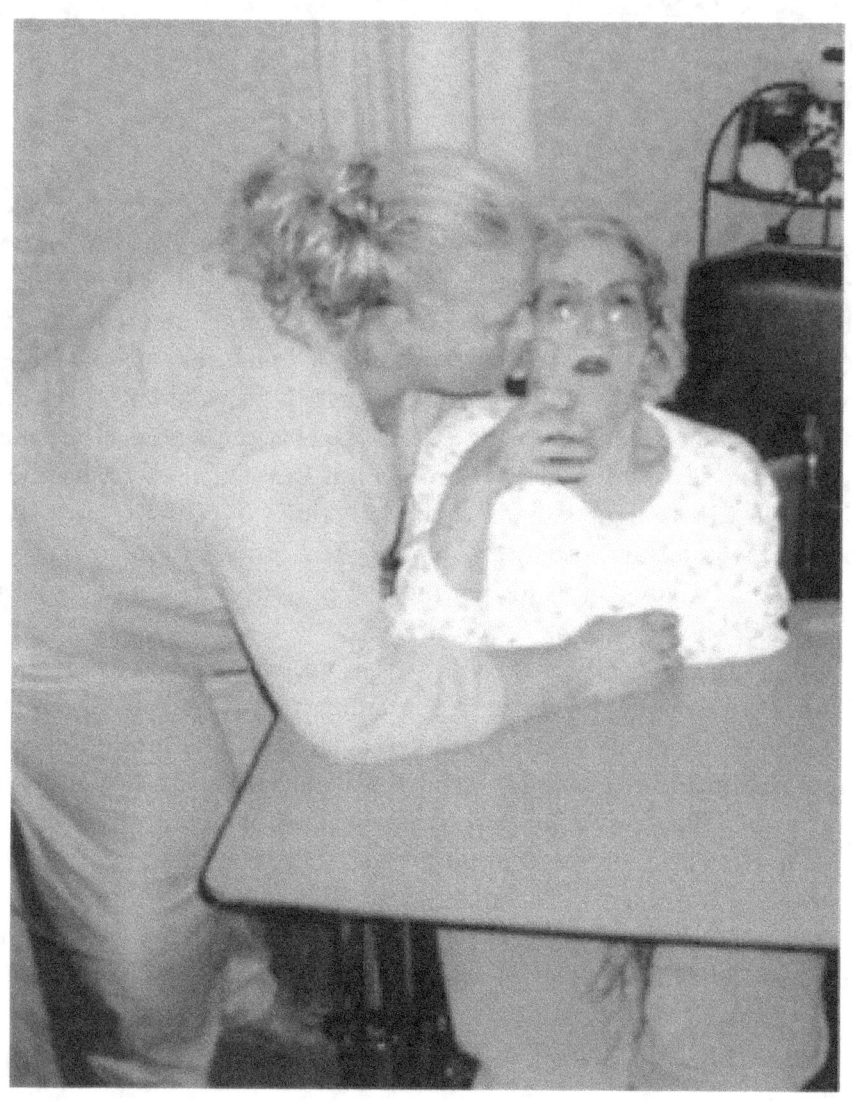

19.

Last plea

EVEN THOUGH MOM, was unable to talk and tell you how she feels. I know that she Knows that something was wrong, mom's health, had took a turn for the worst a feeding Tube was put in, so she could get her medication.

I called my sister who was married to a Baptist preacher and ask her if she would talk To ever one and see if we could all go to the Judge and tell him that there is a big misunderstanding and that our mother is dying and that we all need to be able to stand around mom's bed and tell her that it's ok that we all will meet her in heaven'. She said "Freda, I just don't how I can do that" "I told her that, Jesus, is the answer to any problem that you may have." She still replied, I don't how I can do that. I could not believe this. At least I tried, I can still pray for these people.

20.

Dying mom

M Y BROTHER IN East Valley, Tenn. And told me that mom, was in the dieing process I explained to him sometime this can be fast or it can go on for a few days to a month Until God, gets ready for her. I prayed that God, with his tender mercy's take her under His wing and protect her. I wanted to be there so bad but I didn't in jail. Each time my Brother called, with an update I would pray harder and my church helped me so much. City View Church, Chatsworth, Magnolia my family is still on our church prayer list

After about 2 weeks my brother from East Valley called me and told me that the Nurse said that mom's blood pressure was really low and didn't think that she would make it thru the night. He ask me, "Freda, don't you want to be here? I know you always say that no one should die alone, not even an animal".

I told him that the nurse and the daughter in me would love to be there but at night it's hard to slip in. I told him to go ask the nurse if I could come and the nurse said no. My mom is leaving for heaven and I can't be there. My sisters cheated me out of Earthly visit with my mom, but Thank you Jesus, they can't cheat me out of my They will have no say up there. If they don't get saved they will miss heaven.

My brother told me that he would stay with mom, but told me that he had never been with anyone dying and ask me what he needed to do. I told him she could still hear because hearing the last to go. I told him to talk to her, sing to her read, psalms 23 and 91 say goodbye to her and tell you'll see her in heaven that it's ok to go. She died at 430am. My sister's control ends at the grave I talk to my mom everyday. Her love will always be in my heart.

21.

I NEVER GOT ASKED to help with any arrangements why should I be surprised. I took some pearls and took of my diamond ring and put on her finger. She looked so peaceful but I was so broken hearted. At the funeral home there were flowers and they had names of my sisters on them they were for my sisters not my mom. Oh, well why should I be surprised. On mom's pictures on disk there was my x husband of 20 years can you believe this. But why should I be surprised.

My sisters came up to me at the funeral home and hugged and said, "Freda, I love you." All I could say, was "I don't understand that kind of love, you kept me from my Mother whom I loved so very much." Then they ran away fast saying this isn't the time to discuss this.

The preacher, who was going to do the funeral came up to me and told me that he was going to preach mom's funeral. And told him that he couldn't preach mom's funeral because she had already preached her own. And I told him if could talk to my mom she would tell him to tell everyone if they're not ready to met God. That they would not met my mom in heaven. He said that he would do that.

22.

The Final Good bye

IT WAS SO hard when I woke up the morning of the funeral. I knew that this was it the final good bye. There's no way this could be easy. The preacher, did just what he told me that he would. After the funeral we went to the grave site. After the service at the grave I ask the preacher if I could say something. He told me that I could. So I said, that I was hurting so bad on the inside and outside but at the same time I was rejoicing, because I promise my mom to meet her there.

I also said that I didn't need to mention any names that God, knew who you was and if there was anyone here that had done anything against me and my mom, that I forgive you And I hope that you pray that God for gives you. Nothing more to say –

23.

No MATTER WHAT age we are, we never know what the future holds. With the laws for privacy, it would be very smart to have your wishes in writing and recorded somewhere.

And don't leave anything out. Below are a few questions you might want to have full control of, while you still have your right mind.

1. If something happens to me and I cannot groom myself, would I want someone to help me or letme go?
2. If my heart stops, do I want CPR performed to try to save me?
3. If I am unable to breathe on my own, do I want a machine to help me?
4. Who would be best to handle my money? If possible, get two people. This would be great becausethere would less chance of your money getting used on other things besides just your care.
5. Also, if something happened to me and I couldn't make my own choices, would I want properhealthcare and treatment for my condition?

These questions seem simple but they are very important. Another one might be, DO I WANT ALL MY CHILDREN TO BE ABLE TO TALK TO THEMSELVES ABOUT MY CARE AND TOGETHER, CARRY OUT MY WISHES? IF YOU CAN ANSWER THIS BEFORE SOMETHING HAPPENS, IT WILL SAVE A LOT OF HEARTACHES.

MAY GOD TRULY BLESS EVERYBODY WHO READS THIS BOOK.

Freda Harrison

Our research in Alzheimer's disease gets better each year. It is very important that we don't lose sight of this very important cause. Whenever you see a benefit for this cause, please give as much as you possibly can. Because you or one of your loved ones may get this. Dr. Alois Alzheimer looked at tissue taken from the brain of a woman who had the behavioral symptoms of dementia. He saw microscopic changes called neurotic (senile) plaques and neuron fibrillary tangles. Some of the same structures are found in much smaller numbers in the brains of older people who do not have dementia. Researchers reanalyzed the structure of the chemistry of these plaques and tangles for answers, or for formation and their role in the disease.

Alois Alzheimer was a German physician. In 1907, the disease was named for him. In the past, dementing illnesses of old age were thought to be linked or caused by hardening of the arteries. I know that we all have heard that. Researchers now know that this is not true. In multi-infarct dementia, repeated strokes destroy small areas of the brain. The cumulative effect of this damage leads to dementia. Multi-infarct dementias affect several functions, such as memory, coordination, or speech, but the symptoms differ depending on which areas of the brain are being damaged.

Multi-infarct dementias, in most cases, progress in a step-like way. You may be able to look back and recall that the person was worse after a specific time (instead of the gradual, imperceptible decline in Alzheimer's disease.) Early in the illness, only the memory may be noticeably impaired. They may not be able to do all their actives of daily living, such as remembering how to cook, paying bills, cleaning house, or how to drive. These patients may also become depressed.

Later, impairment in both language and motor skills is really seen. He or she may not be able to do a task which before was so easy. He or she may walk with a stoop or shuffle, or become clumsy. He or she may get lost easily. He or she may become afraid of the dark.

Only your doctor can diagnose Alzheimer's disease, and it is very important to let him know everything that's going on with the patient. Keeping daily notes is a very good idea.

Late in the illness, the patient becomes severely impaired, incontinent, unable to walk, and he or she may fall frequently. Talking becomes a jumble of words, some of which make little or no sense. They may not recognize anyone. This illness leads to death in seven to ten years. But again, only your doctor can diagnose this.

Doctors and scientists group the different things that go on with the brain by their symptoms, just as fever, coughing, vomiting, and dizziness are symptoms of several different diseases, memory loss, confusion, personality changes, and problems with speaking are also symptoms of several different diseases.

Dementia is the medical term for a group of symptoms. It indicates a decline in several areas of intellectual ability, sufficiently severe to interfere with daily functioning in a person who is awake and alert (not drowsy, not intoxicated, or unable to pay attention). This decline in intellectual function means a loss of several kinds of mental processes. It may include changes in personality or not feeling quite as sharp as they used to. THIS DOESN'T MEAN THAT ONE IS DEVELOPING DEMENTIA. REMEMBER, ONLY YOUR DOCTOR CAN TELL FOR SURE.

The symptoms of dementia can also be caused the following.

1. Metabolic disorders.

   Thyroid, parathyroid, or adrenal gland dysfunction; liver or kidney disease; certain vitamin deficiencies such as vitamin B12; Situational problems of the brain; hydrocephalus (abnormal flow of spinal fluid); brain tumors; subdural hematoma (bleeding beneath the skull); trauma; hypoxia and anoxia (little or no enough oxygen reaching the brain); infections; tuberculosis; syphilis; fungal, bacterial and viral infections of the brain (meningitis or encephalitis); acquired immune-deficiency syndrome (AIDS). TOXINS (WHICH ARE POISONS): this happens often with the elderly, because they forget how to take their meds or the caregiver doesn't understand the importance of following doctor's orders. This can also happen to anyone who abuses their meds. Carbon monoxide may also cause dementia. Any drug can cause this, also. Metal poisoning and alcohol, we all know, impairs the brain and we lose brain cells from this.

Degenerative diseases which may cause dementia:
1. Alzheimer's disease
2. Huntington's disease
3. Lewy body dementia
4. Parkinson's disease

5. Front temporal dementia, including Pick's disease.

6. Progressive supranuclear palsy

7. Wilson's disease.

8. Vascular (blood vessel) diseases

9. Stroke or multi-infarct diseases.

10. Binswanger's (subcortical dementia) disease

11. Autoimmune diseases

12. Temporal arteries

13. Lupus erythematosus

14. Psychiatric disorders

15. Depressions

16. Schizophrenia

17. Multiple sclerosis

18. Korsakoff's syndrome is impairment only in memory and not in other mental functions. It isnot a true dementing illness because it only affects one area of mental function.

Again, this is the reason it is so important to keep in touch with the doctor. God is the only miracle cure I know, but he has given our researchers and doctors so much knowledge that all these diseases can be very well managed. The key point is to keep very close contact with your doctor. A lot of this information can be found in *The Lippincott Manual for Nursing Practices*. Also, some came from *Nursing in the Elderly Patients* nursing manual.

24.

A Nurse's Prayer

As I care
For my patients today,
Be there with me
O Lord, I pray,
Make my words kind,
It means so much.
And in my hands,
Place your healing touch.
Let your love shine
Through all I do,
So those in need
May hear and feel you.
Amen.

25.

<u>*Books to Read.*</u>

Mother by Judith Voist

Also the Alzheimer's Association has a book called *The 36 Hour Day*. This book is also a great source of information.

I had run up on a book that caught my eye last Mother's Day. I thought it was the most precious book; it touched my heart. The name of it is *Mothers Are Forever*, by Dr. Criswell Freeman. This is from his book:

> *Our mother interposes herself between us and the*
> *World, protecting us from overwhelming anxiety.*
> *We shall have no greater need than this need for*

THE LORDS PRAYER

OUR FATHER WHO ART IN HAVEN
HALLOWED BE THY NAME
THY KINGDOM COME, THY WILL BE DONE
ON EARTH AS IT IS IN HEAVEN
GIVE US THIS DAY OUR DAILY BREAD
AND FORGIVE US OUR DEBTS
AS WE FORGIVE OUR DEBTORS
AND LEAD US NOT INTO TEMPATIONS
AND DELIVER US FROM EVIL
FOR THINE IS THE POWER
AND GLORY FOREVER
AMEN